Fashion Is Fabulous and Fun

Children's Fashion Books

BABY PROFESSOR

EDUCATION KIDS

What are the latest trends for kids? Let's discover new outfits and really cool attitudes that are trending now. Do you care what you wear? How do you express yourself with fashions?

What is fashion?

Fashion is what we wear and the way we do things. To be "in fashion" is to act and wear clothing in a way that people like at that time. But you have to keep alert, because tastes change and one day you can find yourself "out of fashion".

Fashion changes constantly as it keeps up with the trends and developments of the time.

Clothing fashion is art. It has tremendous power to change people's preferences. What we wear is our personal fashion statement. It suggests who we are and what we want to be.

Our fashion sense is fabulous if it says a lot about us and helps us feel comfortable during the day.

Fashion changes as time passes by. New fashions arise every year.
We get to know the latest trends through famous celebrities.
How they dress creates an impact on our choices and styles.

The latest fashions will be popularized by music, videos, movies, books and TV shows. People want to wear and do what they see famous people wearing and doing.

Children love to wear the latest apparel they see in stores. They love a popular style. Wearing the latest clothing style, footwear, and accessories boosts their confidence and gives them a feeling of being connected with society.

The best fashion
choices for kids will
inspire them to be at
their best. It enhances
of their lifestyle.

Different occasions require a different styles of clothing and behavior. With the help of computers and television, children find it easy to copy or pattern their choices on what are the latest trends.

Fashion is a cool thing in a child's universe. It is can inspire children's moods and help them create fun moments.

Different seasons of the year require fashionable clothing that inspires what your heart desires. For example, when autumn arrives, there will be a parade of warm collections to keep you warm. Hence, nobody gets cold. Online stores will give parents enough choices for their kids. The latest fashion for the autumn will surely keep the kids warm.

The coolest and the most sophisticated brands are what's in fashion. Kids love to have playful and fun new fashions to wear to school or to play with their friends. They love to play with colors.

Fashion is fabulous if it keeps children comfortable and happy. The stores are crowded with light fabrics to keep them cool and comfortable. Cotton fabrics express their moods and catch their attention. Jeans and miniskirts keep them in style and maintain their casual looks.

Pink is fabulous color
that girls really like.
Their world is full of
the gentleness of pink.
It makes them feel
like a princess of their
time. Color in fashion
creates impact that
affects your choices.
Hues of pink imply
purity and romanticism.

Mixing of bright colors such as red, yellow, orange and blue will add modern and innovative looks. Cool combinations of colors in fashion will lead to an exciting result that kids like.

Fashion can help set a holiday mood. Floral dresses highlight any girl's childhood happiness. Iconic fashionable brands are cool things for kids. Sporty jackets will make kids look cool and feel confident. Coveralls and stripes are delightful for kids. Fashion sets the mood of each season.

Why is fashion important?

Fashion is diverse. It's highly dependent on factors such as culture and traditions. Although fashion is sometimes a worldwide trend, every culture still sticks to what is acceptable to their traditions and beliefs that set them apart from others.

But whatever the
latest trend is, fashion
establishes people's
identity, beliefs,
choices, and thoughts
throughout the world.
It creates a great
impact on society and
on relationships.

Visit

BABY PROFESSOR
EDUCATION KIDS

www.BabyProfessorBooks.com

to download Free Baby Professor eBooks
and view our catalog of new and exciting
Children's Books